The GHOST Hunter's Guide

Charles Bouvier

RiverStream

Ever been in bed at night, listening to the floorboards creak as the wood moves and groans, or heard a branch scraping against the window, almost like the long nails of an ancient hand? Deep down, you've probably wondered if that's what they really are...

Ghosts, spirits, wraiths—whatever you call them—are talked about and feared all around the world. From phantom armies to the terrifying yurei of Japan, the White Ladies of the Philippines, the vengeful ghosts bent on luring others to their deaths, and many more, this book tells you how to recognize, and deal with, all kinds of ghost.

Good luck!

Charles Bouvier

CONTENTS

Ghosts Everywhere!

All around the world as night falls, people tell stories of ghosts. Some ghosts are frightening, but harmless. Others can suck the life out of you, or terrify you into insanity.

"She materialized right next to me and she looked like a white mist vaguely in the shape of an old lady. She touched me first on my hand then up on to my arm, and both places she touched me became as cold as ice."

– Account of a haunted grocery store from 1980.

Hunting Ghosts

Ghost hunters are a ghost's worst nightmare. They try to track down these **incorporeal** spirits, before destroying or banishing them. It takes nerves of steel to be a ghost hunter. Very few people are brave enough to pursue ghosts through dusty buildings and lonely woods!

▼ It's always fun telling ghost stories around a campfire—but are you brave enough to go on a ghost hunt afterward?

Becoming A Ghost Hunter

How do you fight a ghost, a creature that can disappear through walls and vanish through closed doors? This book will start you on the path to becoming a ghost hunter.
You'll discover:

- How to tell which ghosts are dangerous.
- The powers ghosts use against their victims.
- Ways to stay safe from ghosts, fight them, and perhaps even destroy them.

▼ Would you be a dedicated enough ghost hunter to visit this spooky house—at night?

Ghost-Hunting Kit

A ghost-hunting kit doesn't need to be expensive. You probably already have many of the things on this list:

- Camera (still and video)
- Sound recorder
- Resealable plastic bags for evidence
- Compass (it starts twitching if there is ghostly energy nearby)
- Talcum powder (for sprinkling and detecting ghostly footprints)
- Thermometer (for confirming drops in temperature).

Ghosts, Spirits, and Revenants

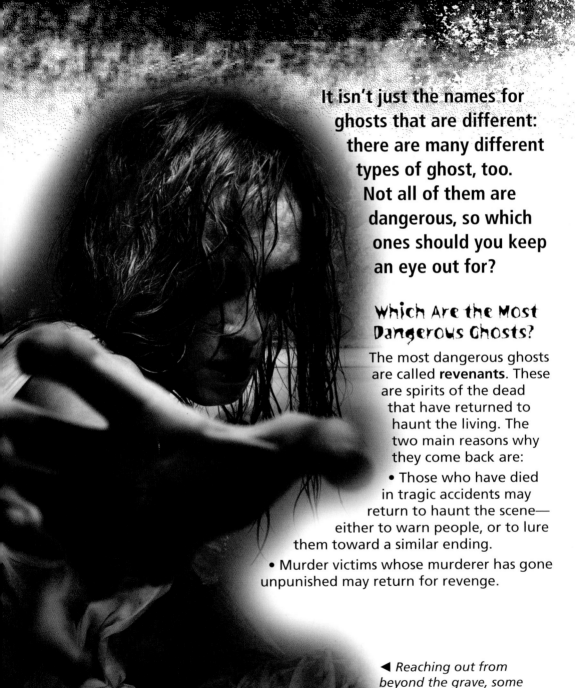

It isn't just the names for ghosts that are different: there are many different types of ghost, too. Not all of them are dangerous, so which ones should you keep an eye out for?

Which Are the Most Dangerous Ghosts?

The most dangerous ghosts are called **revenants**. These are spirits of the dead that have returned to haunt the living. The two main reasons why they come back are:

• Those who have died in tragic accidents may return to haunt the scene—either to warn people, or to lure them toward a similar ending.

• Murder victims whose murderer has gone unpunished may return for revenge.

◄ *Reaching out from beyond the grave, some ghosts are determined to do harm to the living.*

Dangerous Spirits

Around the world, there are plenty of other dangerous ghosts. There are spirits with magical powers and long, sharp teeth. There are "Hungry Ghosts," which have their own special festival each year to stop them from harming the living. And ghost ships, ghost riders, and even ghost armies are regularly seen. So there's plenty to keep a ghost hunter busy!

HAUNTED PLACES

Certain places seem to attract ghosts. For example:
• Beechworth Lunatic Asylum, Australia—haunted by the ghosts of former patients
• Old Ford Motor Factory, Singapore—home to mysterious noises and lights at night
• Union Cemetery, Easton Connecticut—haunted by a White Lady (see pages 10–11), among others.

◄ At the Day of the Dead festival in Mexico, people honor their **ancestors** in the hope that it will stop them from becoming revenants.

▼ Union Cemetery in Easton, Connecticut, is said to be one of the most haunted places in North America.

Lemures of Ancient Rome

Imagine that you're walking along the dark streets of ancient Rome at night. You're looking for robbers, when you catch sight of something out of the corner of your eye. Spinning around, you look toward it— but there's nothing there. Could it be… a lemure?

Ghost Fact File

Name: Lemure
Location: Roman Empire
Age: 2,500 years

▼ The Forum in Rome, Italy, lay at the heart of the city. Thousands of years ago, it was dark and deserted at night. Few dared to cross it for fear of lemures.

Appearance and Behavior

Lemures can be felt most strongly at night. They take no form, and can only be sensed in the shadows, out of the corner of your eye. If they are not banished, they can cause all kinds of trouble:

- Bad luck in business or friendships
- Crops failing or food stores going bad
- Sickness, and even death.

Banishing Lemures

Lemures are best dealt with on May 9, 11, and 13. These are the days when Roman fathers would wait till midnight to scatter handfuls of black beans around the home. The lemures ate the beans, and were satisfied. Any that remained could be scared off by banging bronze pots together.

▲ *Ancient Roman farmers feared angering lemures. If they did, their crops might fail.*

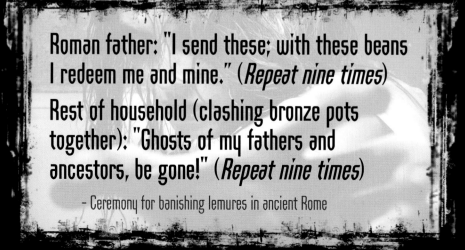

Roman father: "I send these; with these beans I redeem me and mine." (*Repeat nine times*)

Rest of household (clashing bronze pots together): "Ghosts of my fathers and ancestors, be gone!" (*Repeat nine times*)

- Ceremony for banishing lemures in ancient Rome

The White Lady

On lonely roads and paths, late at night, it pays to look out for a White Lady. These mysterious ghosts are unlikely to cause you harm. Instead, they give a warning that something terrible is about to happen.

Ghost Fact File

Name: White Lady
Location: Worldwide
Age: Not known

White Ladies are the ghosts of women who have suffered a tragic death, often after being treated badly by the man they loved. They are often associated with a particular family, and appear before a disaster, usually a death.

▼ *White Lady ghosts appear suddenly on remote, lonely pathways and roads.*

▼ This lonely road in Wyoming has been visited by a White Lady.

Appearance

It is rare to see a White Lady close up, but from a distance she will look exactly as you would imagine. A White Lady is a pale, ghostly woman wearing loose white clothes. White Ladies usually look slightly blurry, especially around the edges.

Behavior

White Ladies rarely hurt the people who see them. Some, having been treated badly by men when alive, are not that happy in male company. If they meet men who remind them of the one they loved, they can get become very disturbed.

WHITE LADIES AROUND THE WORLD

White Lady ghosts appear in many places:
• Berry Pomeroy Castle in Devon, UK
• Mullaghmoyle Road in County Tyrone, Ireland, UK
• Old Faithful Inn in Wyoming (this White Lady has the added characteristic of being headless)
• Balete Drive, Manila, the Philippines.

Ghost Hitchhikers

Imagine yourself in a car on a lonely road, late at night. Suddenly, through the mist and rain, you see a hitchhiker. You pull over, and the hitcher climbs in. But everything is not as it seems. You've just picked up a ghost hitchhiker!

▼ *What was that at the side of the road? It may be safer not to stop to find out!*

Appearance

Ghost hitchhikers look just like any other hitchhiker. But if you meet one, you will probably sense something strange about them. They may not speak much, look pale and ill, or have a strange smell.

RESURRECTION MARY

Mary is the ghost of a young woman buried in Resurrection Cemetery in Chicago. She died after being hit by a car on her way home from a party. Drivers take pity on Mary because she wears only a thin white ballgown. Once in the car, she says nothing until it passes Resurrection Cemetery. "Stop here!" she shouts, then disappears into the graveyard. Only then does the driver realize whom they had picked up....

Behavior

Different ghost hitchhikers rarely behave in exactly the same way. But there are three things that they typically do:

- Disappear from the car the moment it arrives where the hitcher asked to be dropped.
- Get out of the car normally, but leave something behind. When the driver knocks on the door of the house where the hitcher was dropped off, he or she is told that the object belonged to someone who has died.
- Making a **prophecy** of a terrible event, before vanishing into thin air.

▲ *If the Sun's still up, it's probably a real person hitching a ride—not a ghost! Very few ghost hitchhikers appear in daylight.*

Ghostly Crashes

Not all ghost hitchhikers are spooky but harmless. Some evil ghosts seem determined to cause car crashes. There have been many reports of ghosts suddenly appearing in the middle of the road, causing a car to swerve and crash.

▼ *Watch out for ghosts that suddenly appear on a lonely road at night. They are said to cause many accidents.*

Yurei of Japan

Nighttime travelers in the forests of Japan should beware of strange flames that seem to float and flicker through the trees. They may show that a **vengeful**, ghostly yurei is nearby.

Ghost Fact File

Name: Yurei
Location: Japan
Age: Several thousand years

▲ *Could that flickering light between the trees be a yurei?*

A yurei is the spirit of a dead person which can bridge the gap between the **Afterlife** and the physical world. It may come back for revenge, or because of jealousy, hatred, or grief. Or it may have been trapped between the two worlds by not having had a proper burial, being murdered, or dying in tragic circumstances.

Appearance

The yurei almost always appear dressed in white, and have long, black messy hair. Their hands dangle from their wrists, and their arms are held out in front of them, like sleepwalkers. They do not need feet or legs because they move by floating silently through the air.

▲ *A yurei appears before his family, demanding that his spirit be able to rest in peace.*

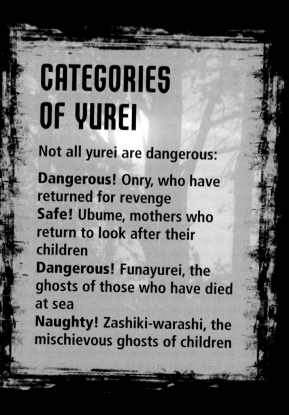

CATEGORIES OF YUREI

Not all yurei are dangerous:

Dangerous! Onry, who have returned for revenge

Safe! Ubume, mothers who return to look after their children

Dangerous! Funayurei, the ghosts of those who have died at sea

Naughty! Zashiki-warashi, the mischievous ghosts of children

Behavior

Yurei are most likely to be seen between 2 and 3 o'clock in the morning, when the barriers between the worlds of the living and the dead are thinnest. They appear near places linked to their death. A yurei who was murdered, for example, will haunt the place where he or she was killed.

There is only one way to get rid of a yurei, and that is to put right whatever caused them to return to the world of the living in the first place. Even then, particularly strong yurei may continue to haunt a place for a long time afterward.

Rakshasa of India

If there's one spirit even the bravest ghost hunter really doesn't want to run into, it is a rakshasa. This spirit from India occupies a physical body. It has a fearsome appearance, poisonous fingernails, and is said to be able to **shape-shift**. If you come across a Rakshasa, run fast!

What Is a Rakshasa?

No one is certain where rakshasas come from. Many people agree, however, that the most dangerous rakshasas are the spirits of those who lived extremely wicked lives.

▲ The crazy staring eyes and fangs are a big clue: this is a rakshasa.

Appearance

Rakshasas are always terrifying to look at, though they are not all identical. Some have ten heads. Others have long, sharp teeth, or are almost 20 feet (6 meters) tall. All, though, are scary enough to make the blood drain from your face. And they are spectacularly bad tempered.

"Rakshasa is the [follower] of Ravana. Ravana, whose deeds were so horrible they stopped the Sun and Moon in their course."

– from Kolchak: The Night Stalker (1974)

Behavior

Generally, rakshasas are not very well behaved. Their favorite activities include:

• Making a mess of graves.
• Eating human flesh.
• Taking **possession** of human beings and making them perform evil acts.
• Disrupting religious ceremonies.

Each rakshasa has magical powers, and is a master of illusion. This makes them extremely hard to beat— though Hindu stories do tell of the defeat of the rakshasa leader Ravana and his followers in a great battle.

▼ *Rakshasas are the followers of Ravana, the Hindu demon, who snarls out from this carving.*

Noisy Spirits

You're in a house investigating a haunting. Suddenly, a heavy chair starts to move across the room. It stops, but then there's a noise of banging from the kitchen—a room with no one in it. Finally, an invisible hand throws a book at your head. It's time to leave! You've stumbled across a poltergeist.

AMITYVILLE

In 1975, a family named Lutz moved into a house in Amityville, New York State. A year earlier, the house had been the scene of a terrible murder.

Terrifying events began to happen:
• Swarms of flies would appear.
• Red eyes were seen looking out of the windows.
• Green slime oozed from the walls, and through keyholes.

The events were blamed on a poltergeist. In January 1976, the Lutz family moved out, and never returned.

▲ *The house on 112 Ocean Drive, where the Amityville haunting is said to have taken place.*

▲ A scene from the 1982 movie Poltergeist, in which a young girl is haunted by ancient ghosts.

Appearance

Poltergeists are rarely visible. You will know that there is a poltergeist around though. Poltergeist means "noisy spirit," and this ghost certainly makes itself heard. Strange noises are common when there's a poltergeist around, including mysterious footsteps, the sound of furniture being moved in empty rooms, and unexplained crashes and bangs.

Behavior

Poltergeists are known as evil spirits, rather than ghosts. They are often linked to a particular human, usually a young woman, who becomes the focus of the poltergeist's actions, and are usually, though not always, associated with a particular place. Poltergeists are angry, disruptive ghosts. They throw things around, make a lot of noise and mess, and may even attack people.

Getting Rid of a Poltergeist

Poltergeists usually appear suddenly, and disappear just as quickly. People have tried using a religious ceremony called **exorcism** to get rid of poltergeists. Usually, though, the poltergeist eventually goes away of its own accord.

Ghost Ship: The Flying Dutchman

You might think that the last thing sailors want to observe far out at sea is a terrible storm approaching. In fact, that's the second-to-the-last thing. The very LAST thing sailors want to see is a ghost ship called *The Flying Dutchman*.

Ghost Fact File

Name: *The Flying Dutchman*
Location: Any ocean
Age: At least 300 years

A Dreadful Omen

The *Dutchman*, as sailors call it, is known to be a **harbinger** of bad luck. Some kind of dreadful disaster or accident always befalls those who see it—usually a shipwreck. That's why sailors hope to never see the *Flying Dutchman* appear on the horizon.

◄ *An old painting showing the The Flying Dutchman (far left) luring a sailing ship to its doom on the rocks.*

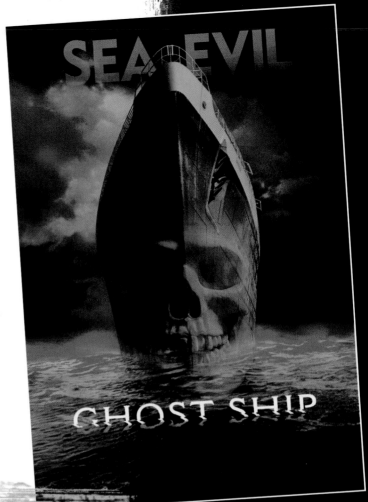

SEA EVIL

GHOST SHIP

► *The 2002 movie Ghost Ship, in which people are trapped on a ship, was partly inspired by the legend of the Flying Dutchman.*

THE LEGEND of the FLYING DUTCHMAN

The *Dutchman* was commanded by Captain Van der Drecken. When the captain was asked to put into port instead of continuing to fight a fierce wind off of South Africa, he replied: "I will round this Cape even if I have to keep sailing till **Doomsday!**" Soon after, the ship was wrecked, but Van der Drecken's ghost ship is still said to sail the high seas, and will do until the world ends.

Appearance and Behavior

The *Dutchman* is a sailing ship dating from the 1700s. According to legend, it was wrecked while sailing around the stormy Cape of Good Hope off of South Africa. From a distance, the ship glows with a ghostly light.

The whole ship appears wrecked and ruined, and only tattered sails hang from its masts. Despite its shredded sails, the *Dutchman* is often reported sailing against the wind, as if driven by some magical power.

Phantom Armies

There is a scene in the movie trilogy *The Lord of the Rings* where one of the characters summons a **phantom** army to help him in a great battle. Of course, *The Lord of the Rings* is based on a story—but there have been plenty of reports of phantom armies in real life, too.

◄ *A ghostly army appears out of the misty forest. How could you defeat such enemies, when they're already dead?*

Appearance

It is usually possible to tell you are looking at a ghost army, rather than a real one. They often come from an earlier time, and are dressed differently from modern soldiers. But some ghost armies are very convincing. In 1746, villagers near Souter **Fell** in England fled from an army of Scottish soldiers invading England—only to realize later that it was a ghost army.

Behavior

Ghost armies generally limit their activities to appearing and disappearing. But some are said to have taken part in actual fighting:

• Ghost armies twice saved the Italian city of Otranto from capture by Turkish forces. When the city was attacked in 1537 and 1644, the ghosts of 800 soldiers killed in an earlier battle with the Turks appeared.

• During the Battle of Mons (part of the World War I, 1914–18), a force of spirits rescued English soldiers from certain death by startling the horses of their German attackers, giving the English a chance to escape.

▼ *Spooky Denbigh Moors is said to be regularly visited by ghost armies.*

Civil War Armies

Phantom armies have appeared at battle sites from the English **Civil War** (1642–51), and the American Civil War (1861–65). They include:

• Edgehill, Naseby, and Roundway Down in England

• Shiloh in Tennessee, where there are regular reports of phantom armies and mysterious sounds of battle.

THE HAUNTED MOOR

Denbigh Moors, in north Wales, is said to be haunted both by a ghostly Roman **centurion**, and a 3,000-strong army from the 1800s. It's a spooky place: strange noises, odd lights, and UFOs have all been reported there too.

China's Hungry Ghost Festival

Ghost Fact File

Name: Hungry Ghost
Location: China and South-
    East Asia
Age: At least 2,000 years

The seventh month of the Chinese calendar is a great time for a ghost hunter to visit China. For the whole month, dead souls return to the world of the living as ghosts.

Some of these ghosts may be "hungry"—wanting something from the living. Unless they are kept happy, they may cause bad luck, sickness, or even unexpected deaths. The Hungry Ghost festival aims to make the ghosts contented, so that they bring good luck instead of bad.

▲ People burn offerings to the spirits to celebrate the Hungry Ghost festival.

The Most Ghostly Day

On the fifteenth day of the seventh month, according to Chinese legend, the gates between Heaven, Hell, and the world of the living are wide open, and ghosts can pass between them. There are several ways to keep wandering ghosts from causing harm:
• Putting on shows to entertain them (but NEVER sit in the front row—it's reserved for ghosts!).
• Preparing complicated meals, with places set for dead ancestors.
• Burning paper models of golden materials, fine clothes, paper money, and other precious things, as gifts to the dead.

"People pray for their dead ancestors, and hope they do not come up to haunt them or their loved ones. They are also very careful in doing almost anything [risky], i.e. no fast driving, no swimming, etc."
– Felix from Taiwan.

GHOST FESTIVALS AROUND THE WORLD

Even though the Hungry Ghost festival is Chinese, it is also celebrated in Japan (where it is called O-bon), Vietnam (Tét Trung Nguyên), and anywhere else around the world in countries with large Chinese communities.

▶ *Chinese god Hu Fa Shi Zhe is an important spirit to keep happy— he is the controller of ghosts and devils.*

All Hallows' Eve

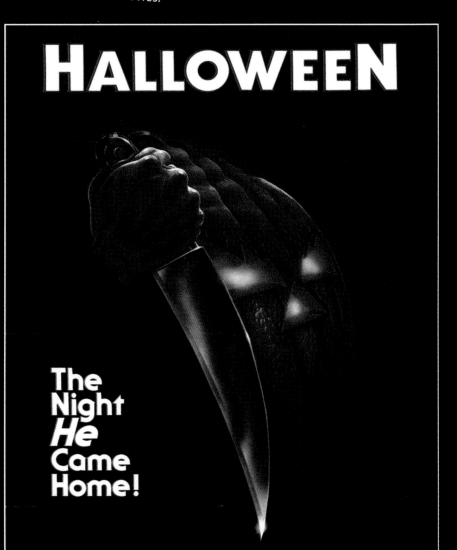

All Hallows' Eve is usually called Halloween. People dress up in costumes and go trick-or-treating, knocking on doors in the hope that they'll be given candies. But All Hallows' Eve has a much more sinister, ghostly past.

▼ *Halloween has been the subject of plenty of horror movies.*

HALLOWEEN

The
Night
He
Came
Home!

For centuries, people have known that on All Hallows' Eve, the walls between the worlds of the living and the dead are at their thinnest. This is when evil spirits are free to visit the world of the living.

Trick-or-Treating

When you knock on someone's door trick-or-treating, you're continuing an ancient tradition. It started many years ago, when poor people would call at the homes of the rich, asking for food. In return they would pray for the souls of the dead, so that they did not come back to haunt the living.

Halloween Costumes

Dressing up in scary costumes is a kind of "guising." "Guising" means disguising yourself as a ghost or demon in the hope that you will fool the evil sprits into thinking you are one of them, and leaving you alone.

Jack o'Lanterns

Jack o'lanterns are traditionally lit on Halloween. They are a reminder of Stingy Jack, a miserly Irish farmer who tried to cheat on a deal with the Devil. As a result he was cursed to wander the Earth forever, using a candle inside a hollowed-out turnip to light his way.

"'Tis now the very witching time of night,
When churchyards yawn and hell itself breathes out
Contagion to this world."
- from *Hamlet* (William Shakespeare)

▼ *Old stories say that snaggle-toothed lanterns like these are lit on All Hallows' Eve to keep evil spirits such as Stingy Jack away.*

Ghosts on screen

Nearly everyone enjoys feeling scared
once in a while—as long as we're just not
too scared! And one of the best ways to
get your scary thrills is to go to and see
a ghost movie.

Old-School Movies

Old ghost movies were made in the days
before filmmakers could really use
special effects. Instead, the audience
had to imagine what might be
creeping up on the actors. Some
of the best ones include:

• *The Uninvited* (1944)—
A brother and sister buy a
mysterious, abandoned
house, and strange things
start to happen…

• *The Haunting* (1963)—
the simple story of four
guests invited to spend
the night in a house, to
prove that ghosts and
spirits do not exist. Of
course, it turns out that
perhaps they do…

▶ *A scary scene from one
of the best ghost movies
of all time*—The Haunting.

"An evil old house, the kind some people call haunted... Silence lay steadily against the wood and stone of Hill House, and whatever walked there—walked alone."

– Dr. John Markway in The Haunting (1963).

◄ There's nothing like the thrill of a ghost movie. Just make sure you don't walk alone along a dark path home from the movie theater!

▲ In Sleepy Hollow, *Constable Ichabod Crane gets tangled up with a ghostly Headless Horseman.*

Modern Ghost Movies

Modern ghost movies are sometimes quite bloodthirsty. But there are some great movies that manage to be scary without being too gory:

• *The Sixth Sense* (1999)—the story of a young boy who sees and speaks with ghosts.

• *Ghostbusters* (1984)—not so much scary as funny, this movie tells the story of a team of crack ghost trackers and their efforts to stop evil spirits from destroying the world.

• *Sleepy Hollow* (1998)—the story of police constable Ichabod Crane, and his attempts to get rid of the Headless Horseman.

Technical Information

Words from this Book:

Afterlife
place where the spirits of the dead go.

ancestor
person who lived a long time ago.

centurion
soldier in the army of ancient Rome.

civil war
war fought between two sides who are from the same country.

contagion
harm and decay.

Doomsday
in Christian beliefs, the day at the end of the world when people will be judged and sent to heaven or hell.

exorcism
religious ceremony to get rid of ghosts.

fell
area of high ground.

harbinger
messenger or announcer.

incorporeal
without a body.

manifest
appear or reveal.

phantom
old word for a ghost or spirit.

possession
control or ownership.

prophecy
a forecast or prediction. Ghosts, with their connections to the spirit world, seem to be able to know the future as well as the past, and sometimes make prophecies.

revenant
spirit of a dead person, which has returned to the world of the living (often to avenge an injustice).

shape-shift
change shape or form.

vengeful
wanting to take revenge.

Equipment:

Basic ghost-hunting equipment is listed on page 5. The following items are more specialized, and may be very expensive. They're for expert ghost trackers only!

Electromagnetic frequency (EMF) detector—these pick up electronic fields (which may be given off by ghosts) at various frequencies.

Infrared scanner (hand-held)—this picks up infrared light. Some ghosts may be seen using infrared light, or may give it off.

Night-vision equipment—goggles help you to see what's happening in the dark; night-vision cameras will record events.

More Ghostly Information

Other Books

Ghosts and Monsters: Frightening Phantoms and Supernatural Spooks (TickTock Books, 2006)
Collected information about all kinds of ghosts, plus other supernatural events.

Encyclopedia Horrifica: The Terrifying Truth About Vampires, Ghosts, Monsters, and More Joshua Gee (Scholastic, 2007)
Not just ghosts, but all kinds of supernatural and paranormal creatures and events, are covered in this fact-filled book.

The Encyclopedia of the Unexplained Judy Allen (Kingfisher, 2006)
Although the section on ghosts doesn't take up much of this book, it's still a good read. The rest, which deals with mysteries such as crop circles and the Bermuda Triangle, is really interesting, too!

Although the following are adult titles, they would be useful to confident readers who want to find out more:

The Mammoth Book of True Hauntings & The Mammoth Book of Haunted House Stories both Peter Haining (Robinson, 2008)
These books are absolutely jam-packed with examples of hundreds of hauntings from around the world.

The Paranormal: Caught On Film Melvyn Willin (David & Charles, 2008)
Some brilliant photographs of what may, or may not, be ghosts.

The Internet

www.monstropedia.org
This is a great big rambling site, which is absolutely full of information about all kinds of weird, supernatural, and scary creatures. To get to the ghosts section, click on "Paranormal entities," then "Ghosts."

www.ghostresearch.org/ghostpics/
This site is great fun—some maybe-ghost photos, and some that everyone admits are fakes, with explanations of how they can be faked. Click on "Typical web site frauds" for some really good ones.

Movies and DVDs

Beetlejuice (1988, dir. Tim Burton)
A darkly funny movie about a dead couple who decide to hang around their old house in order to scare away the new inhabitants.

Ghostbusters (1984, dir. Ivan Reitman)
A comedy movie (with some great tunes in it) about a trio of men who set up a business to rid New York of its ghosts and ghouls.

Index

Hardcover library-bound edition first published
in 2012 by

Sea-to-Sea Publications
Distributed by Black Rabbit Books
P.O. Box 3263, Mankato, Minnesota 56002
www.blackrabbitbooks.com

Copyright © Sea-to-Sea Publications 2012

Printed in China

All rights reserved.

9 8 7 6 5 4 3 2

RiverStream Publishing reprinted by arrangement
with the Watts Publishing Group Ltd, London.

Series editor: Adrian Cole
Art director: Jonathan Hair
Design: Mayer Media
Picture research: Diana Morris

A CIP catalog record for this book
is available from the Library of Congress.

ISBN: 978-1-59771-316-0 (library binding)
ISBN: 978-1-59771-344-3 (eBook)

February 2011
RD/6000006415/001

1 2 3 4 5 CG 15 14 13 12

RiverStream Publishing—Corporate Graphics,
Mankato, MN—122012—1009CGW12
Paperback version printed in the USA

Acknowledgements:
Art Archive: 22b. Asia Images Group/Alamy: 16b. Blitznetsov/
Shutterstock: 1, 4c, 6, 9b, 17c, 25t, 29t. Sascha Burkard/
istockphoto: 5t, 7tr, 11t, 11b, 12b,15b, 23c, 25c. Jeff Chiasson/
istockphoto: 29c. Compass International/Kobal Collection:
26b. Mary Evans PL/Alamy: 15t. Ekaterina Fribus/Shutterstock:
27. Eddie Gerald/Alamy: 13t. Jpse Gil/Shutterstock: 7c. Chris
Harvey/Fotolia: front cover. Chris Hellier/Alamy: 25b. Roger
Holmes/Getty Images: 23b. Iconspro/Shutterstock: 2. Ivancovlad/
Shutterstock: 8c, 10t, 14c, 16t, 20t, 24t. Neal & Molly Jansen/
Alamy: 10b. Geoffrey Jewett/Shutterstock: 4tl, 8tl, 12tl,
14tl, 18tl, 22tl, 26tl. Rob Johnson: 7b. P Kirill /Shutterstock:
12c. Natalia Lukiyanova/frenta/Shutterstock: 3. Maodesign/
istockphoto: 5b. MGM/AF Archive/Alamy: 19t. MGM/Kobal
Collection: 28. Syamsui Bahri Muhammad/Getty Images: 24b.
North Wind PA/Alamy: 20b.Graham Oliver/Alamy: 17b. Silvia
Otte/Getty Images: 8b. Paramount/Mandalay/Kobal Collection:
29b. Picturepoint/Topham: 18b. David Ponton/Corbis: 14b.
Quavondo/istockphoto: 13b. Corey Rich/Aurora Photos/Alamy:
4b. Warner Brothers/Kobal Collection: 21t. Gari Wyn Williams/
Alamy: 9c.

Every attempt has been made to clear copyright.
Should there be any inadvertent omission please
apply to the publisher for rectification.